Bushido
The Samurai Code of Honor

The Truth about Japanese Samurai Wisdom

What Samurai Philosophy Can Teach You in Modern Life

DINGO
B O O K   C L U B

"Great Books Change Life"

Table of Contents

Introduction

Inazo Nitobe describes the code of the Samurai best. With flowery language and a scholarly viewpoint that is the epitome of gentlemen educators, Nitobe has given the modern world an answer to what it means to examine the Samurai, the Bushido, and apply this to the contemporary world.

A phrase commonly stated today is, "Chivalry is dead." Anytime a man opens a door and does not hold it for a lady or whenever he does not get out and open the car door first. When man forgets to use manners in front of women, "chivalry is dead."

For some scholars, it never existed. However, for Nitobe, the code of the Samurai was genuine, and it managed to live on well after the Western world let go of the feudal system.

Bu-shi-do translates into English as "Military-Knight-Ways," not a very elegant translation, and chivalry is considered "horsemanship," which also does not lend itself to the power of such codes as people lived by.

Bushido is a "code of moral principles" which men were supposed to follow through instruction or requirement. It is not something that is "written" but is instead a belief handed down orally throughout the feudal times. Yes, some attempted to write it, but how can one describe what is unwritten and unuttered in most circles? The heart is where the Bushido code lives on, with more than one brain or single person giving life to the ethics one should follow.

This code gave rise to the Samurai, a professional class of warriors strong enough to survive battles, start families and gain significant honor. The Bu-ke or Bu-shi were fighting knights, with Samurai rising to high ranks of privilege and honor, taking on enormous responsibility. It was necessary for these men to have a standard of behavior to separate themselves from the "brutes" written about as nothing more than savages by the English. It was necessary for the Samurai to have a final judgment on any misdeeds to hold in check the rude behaviors of lesser people, not worthy of being in the same ranks.

Living beyond the Samurai during Feudal Japan, meant protecting their way of life from invading forces, and certain aspects of the code still exist. These morals are seen in the customs of Japanese people, how they act towards others and work to support their families.

Military personnel is still necessary, and perhaps we can see the Samurai live on in the teachings they gain. After all, the Samurai and Bushido code existed to ensure Japan was safe. It stands to reason that this history of military prowess lives on, in the military as it does in other aspects of regular life.

Discover what Bushido and the Samurai Code of Honor are really about. Find the correlations that can apply to your life and the world you live in. Perhaps, you will see there are great lessons to be gained.

Chapter 1:
History of the Samurai

The Samurai may have been warriors of premodern Japan, but their legacy lives on in the Bushido code. These men rose high in military ranking and eventually became the highest-ranking class. The Edo period, between 1603 and 1867, was the best era for the bushi. These great warriors were able to wield bows, arrows, spears and guns. However, it was their swords they were most known for and what continues to symbolize their heritage.

To understand the code or the way of the warrior, you need to know that many of the men in the military followed Confucian teachings and Zen Buddhism. Both schools of thought are what taught the men to be respectful, have self-discipline and that loyalty and ethical behavior were a must.

Depending on which scholar you ask, the warriors of Japan did not begin their existence until the Heian period (794-1185). A battle between different lineages of Japanese, like the Emishi people in Tohoku showed a need for men with fighting skills.

Wealthy landowners also needed protection against armies. These owners were independent of the central government but were allowed to build armies. The two most powerful clans were Taira and Minamoto. They also created their armies to rise against the government and each other.

You should recognize Minamoto Yoritomo from the Minamoto clan. He was victorious over the government and established a new one in 1192, based on military laws. The military government was led by a supreme military commander, called a shogun. It is this battle that helped the Samurai rule Japan for close to 700 years.

These 700 years are where many of the films by Kurosawa have come from, depicting the code of the Samurai and ninja warriors. The most chaotic period was between the 15th and 16th centuries, with many warring states fighting to have supremacy over others. Japan became states or prefectures, with distinct differences in ruling styles and laws, but one thing was in common—warriors of high skills. Whether the warriors became Samurai or ninjas, it was a time when different skills evolved giving rise to the fictional depictions we know today.

At the tail end of the 15th century, Japan became united again, with a social caste system. It was an unbending system that put the Samurai at the top, with farmers, artisans, and merchants below them. The shogun made the Samurai live in the castle towns, carrying the only swords. The ruling shogun decided that no one, other than warriors, could have swords and raids occurred to remove all weapons from farmers and people below them in ranking.

Samurai earned rice given by their feudal lords or daimyo. Not all Samurai had masters. Some, known as ronin, left the ranks, and wandered, sometimes causing minor troubles in the 1600s.

The power of the Samurai was well known, which allowed peace to win against more massive wars during the Edo period. Unfortunately, martial arts skills declined due to a lack of need, and many Samurais started taking other jobs in the government, becoming teachers, or artists. By 1868, the feudal era ended and soon after the need for the Samurai class disappeared, and with it the abolishment of their caste.

Origins of the Samurai

Scholars have traced the origins of the Samurai to the Kanto plain, although not all of the men came from this area, the original warriors did. The Kanto plain is in the south of Japan, and these men worked on their skills to fight the Emishi. At first, the Samurai was considered nothing special, other than their qualifications they worked on. They were rowdy, even barbarian-like, but it was realized a code was necessary to bring their reputation up a notch and increase their status amongst their peers and masters.

Bravery on the battlefield is one element of the Samurai that increased in prowess throughout history. Their traditions with battle cries and challenging single enemies to combat, showed that these men were fearless and filled with honor.

There are different levels in the Samurai system. The gokenin or housemen was the lowest rank and the vassals of feudal lords. Goshi were rustic warriors who could farm their land, but until they reached full Samurai rank, they could not own swords. The Hatamoto or bannermen were the highest-ranking members capable of holding swords, being a part of the government, and owning land.

Despite the prowess and eventual rise to top the caste system in Feudal Japan, the Samurai was only six percent of the population. Part of holding such a high rank meant they could kill anyone without legal repercussions, but their code also instilled certain virtues that ensured they did so when they were in the right.

Samurai also had assistants known as baishin. These assistants worked the land for their masters. When war needed the men away from home, the baishin would take care of the property. But, with the rules about swords, the areas were left defenseless when Samurai was gone. It meant leaving a few behind that could defend the territory.

In some instances, the women were able to defend their masters' land. A small group of female warriors did exist, but they were called onna bugeisha and were not Samurai. The words translate as martially-skilled women.

Samurai Dress and Weapons

Samurai were horse owners. They would ride into battle on horses, fighting with bows and arrows to take out as many enemies from a distance as possible. Their swords were long with a curved blade. They also carried shorter swords by the 1500s. Hideyoshi decreed that they needed this second shorter sword. However, it was only the full Samurai who could hold the two swords.

Samurai preferred to attack at night as a way of surprising the enemy.

For their dress, they wore silk cloaks called horo, which would fasten at the neck and the waist. The armor was leather and light to make it easier to move. The armor found in most museums outside of Japan came from later periods, usually the 17th century. The armor pieces were more substantial in the 1700s than in earlier centuries.

The Japanese sword is known as the katana. It is a curved sword, with a blade of 60 centimeters. The blade was single edged, with a slender metal. It also had a circular or square guard between the handle. The grip accommodated two hands. There is also the tachi that was used by earlier Samurai. The sword was more curved than the katana. The tachi was worn with the cutting edge down, while the katana had the cutting edge up. The katana is considered one of the best in history for cutting, since they were reputed to cut steel in half. Of course, they could not, but a piece of silk falling from a short height could be cut in half.

When it comes to the sword names of Japan the Jokoto was first, being used until 900 CE. The Koto came next as the sword of choice, until 1596. The Shinto was used from 1596 to 1780. Newer swords were the Shinshinto, Gendaito, and Shinsakuto. It is the Shinsakuto that are made today. You should also understand that the katana was a word to describe the long sword, but the different names like Shinto were also used depending on the time period. Samurai had katana blades for most of their battles, using shorter swords for seppuku and closer combat. The fact is that the sword was carried as a sign of honor, and not all men would use them. The skill of the Samurai would depend on what weapon he chose to wield.

Seppuku

Anyone who has seen a Samurai movie understands the word seppuku, but was it a concept? Yes, it is true that the Samurai was expected to fight to their death if necessary. To prevent capture, a Samurai could kill himself. It was an honor to perform seppuku rather than to be executed by an enemy after being captured. Seppuku was a form of self-disembowelment. The Samurai believed the spirit was contained in the stomach area and not the heart. The ritual required the Samurai to wear a white robe, for purity, cut his abdomen with a knife from left to right. Once the cut in the stomach occurred, there was an assistant that would decapitate the Samurai. The Kaishakunin was a special sword for this purpose. Bleeding to death by a cut to the abdomen was slow and painful, thus the reason for the assistant. Retainers of the Samurai would then have to commit suicide because of their master's death. It was a code called junshi or death by following.

Several Samurais make up the legends and myths of Japan. Many of the people in these legends were real but have been mythologized.

Chapter 2:
Famous Samurai Warriors

The most famous Samurai in history is Minamoto-no-Yoshitsune, originally named Ushiwakamaru. He lived from 1159 to 1189. Yoshitsune was the younger brother of a shogun who fought in the Gempei War. Legend says he was honorable, loyal, and unflappable. He learned to fence in his adolescent years, fought robbers to stop them from hurting people in the countryside, and even gained Benkei, a warrior monk as his servant.

Yoshitsune won several battles like the Ichinotani fight, where he supposedly leaped onto a boat bridge at Danno-Ura helping to end the fight. It is said his brother's jealousy rose at his conquests and due to discord, Yoshitsune ran across the border of Benkei, where he was beaten. The myth says his brother found him, blockaded a castle, and burned it to the ground killing Yoshitsune. Some say he escaped and was Temujin, the Mongol prince known as Genghis Khan; other stories say he died in the fire. The Noh and Kabuki theatre was known for telling this warrior myth.

Forty-Seven Ronin

The Forty-Seven Ronin, which was depicted by pop culture movie *The Ronin*, is based on a story of honor and real-life occurrence. The Shikushichishi occurred in 1703. Asano Naganor, lord of Ako, was at a castle in Edo and insulted by Kira Yoshinaka. Being offended Asano drew his sword inside the walls of the castle, which was a capital offense. For this wrong, he had to commit seppuku, and his 47 followers or Ronin swore revenge on Kira for this death. They became Ronin because they no longer had a master. For two years, they waited, finally killing Kira Yoshinaka, and decapitating him, leaving the head on the grave of their Samurai master. The Ronin were forced to face a public debate and told they could perform seppuku. For some reason, the story shows that 46 men between 15 and 77 accepted seppukus and gained legendary status. The missing person is unaccounted for, and the history books do not show who it might have been. The Ronin were honored in their burial, being placed inside the Sengakuji Temple with their master.

The two stories above are just a small portion of the Samurai who rose to fame throughout history. There are another twelve who deserve a bit of time.

Ten Shoguns and Warriors

The list of warriors and Shoguns is a compilation of men who not only made a mention in scholarly articles but also gained recognition through statues in Japan. You will hear about many of these men when you visit.

Shimazu Yoshihisa was a warrior from the Satsuma province. He was known for marrying his aunt for a short time, as was a custom for a woman during those times when women needed to be protected. He was also responsible for launching a campaign to unify Kyushu. He ruled Kyushu, but Toyotomi Hideyoshi eventually defeated him. Instead of dying from seppuku he was able to live out his life as a Buddhist monk and died a peaceful death. This was not always the case for men of this time; many perished in war or because of the Bushido code.

Date Masamune is another Samurai that lived an honorable life. He was first known for violence and no mercy. Several Samurais of his era feared him. One of the interesting facts is that he did not have any sight in his right eye due to a bout of smallpox as a child. He built a reputation for being fierce, even slaughtering his enemies when they kidnapped his father. He served Toyotomi and Tokugawa, who became the head of his Date clan.

The Dragon of Echigo was Uesugi Kenshin. This man was another fierce warrior, who led the Nagao clan. His most famous situation was with Takeda Shingen. The two tribes fought for years, with one on one combats, waged to show their prowess against each other. Kenshin resisted Oda Nobunaga. Several myths surround his death, but it is known that he was a fair administrator in the government.

Tokugawa Leyasu was an ally of Nobunaga and later the successor for Toyotomi Hideyoshi. His prowess was in brains versus the blade. When Hideyoshi died, it was Tokugawa who raised an army to defeat the enemies and ensure his clan would rule. The Battle of Sekigahara waged in 1600 was won by him. He was also the first person to be named Shogun. His legacy the Tokugawa shogunate provided a time of peace, until his death in 1868.

Hattori Hanzo was a rare Samurai because he was also trained as a ninja and the leader of the Iga Clan. He was a servant of Leyasu, saving his master from death numerous times. Hanzo used the spear versus the sword or bow in battle. He lived to become a Buddhist monk. Today, Hanzo lives on as a fictional warrior in pop culture.

Takeda Shingen or the Tiger of Kai was a poet and fierce warrior. In the fourth battle of Kawanakajima, he fought Uesugi Kenshin in a one on one battle. He also had success against Oda Nobunaga. Shingen was one of the only Samurais to have had the power to stop Nobunaga. However, in 1573, he died, and Nobunaga was able to consolidate the power of his tribe into his own.

Honda Tadakatsu was the "warrior who surpassed death." He was also one of the "Four Heavenly Kings of Tokugawa." It is said he played a part in over a hundred fights and was never defeated in any of them. He used the Dragonfly cutter, which was a spear, rather than a sword. His statue shows him with the spear and dragon horns. Tadakatsu was part of the Battle of Sekigahara and helped bring a new era to Japan because of his involvement.

Miyamoto Musashi is one of the most celebrated warriors of Japan. He was reputed to be the best or at least close to the best swordsmen. His first duel was when he was thirteen. He also fought during the battle of the Toyotomi and Tokugawa clans. He was defeated in that battle; however, he lived on to travel throughout Japan, winning duels. In 1612, he was part of the most famous duel with the master swordsman, Sasaki Kojiro. Kojiro died. He is notable for the *Book of the Five Rings*, as well as other writings. The book is about sword fighting techniques.

Toyotomi Hideyoshi succeeded Oda Nobunaga to become ruler and top warrior during his era. Hideyoshi was a peasant who rose in the ranks due to his skill on and off the battlefield. He ruled from 1585 to 1598 but was never given the Shogun title. He was responsible for creating the Osaka Castle, as well as waging and winning wars with China and Korea. His clan was taken out after his death.

This entire discussion has been leading up to one of the most famous Samurai—Oda Nobunaga. He was a charismatic person, capable of driving his people and keeping much of Japan united. He killed Yoshimoto Imagawa in 1560, merging Japan and stopping Imagawa from taking over Kyoto. Oda liked firearms and used them in battle. His death was a betrayal of Akechi Mitsuhide, a general in his army. Mitsuhide started a fire at a temple, where Oda was resting. Nobunaga was defeated in battle and committed seppuku rather than face the less honorable death by the winner of the fight.

These are the men who are living on through writing, pop culture, manga, anime, and the myths of their epic battles. There are certainly more men who fought as Samurai that are not mentioned, and some are no less than the great men in this section. It is just the names here are those who remain affixed in the public eye because of their statues and feats.

Chapter 3:
The Eight Virtues of Bushido

The Samurai, according to Nitobe, followed an ethical system, which constituted eight virtues. These qualities have an emphasis on compassion, benevolence, and non-martial arts qualities that show what a true gentleman and warrior is. Learning these eight elements will help in applying the Code of Bushido to modern life.

The Virtues

1. A Samurai has martial arts knowledge and personal integrity. It is the most robust code of the Bushido. According to Nitobe, "Rectitude is one's power to decide upon a course of conduct," it is within reason, without ever wavering, and dying when dying is correct. It is also about striking the enemy when it is right. Another Samurai said it is a "firmness and stature." It is not talent or learning, but the bones of a person, since a human's head cannot rest without the spine or move without hands and feet.

2. Courage is different from bravery, according to the code. Courage knows when to exercise righteousness and rectitude. Confucius stated

that one could perceive what is right and not lack courage because courage is doing what is morally correct. An example for today would be someone stealing money from work and seeing it. Perceiving what is right is reporting this issue and having the courage to follow through. Sometimes doing the right thing is about inaction and at other times it requires facing the more difficult path.

3. Mercy or Benevolence is the second code of honor, in which a man invests in the power to command and kill, with equal powers of compassion and benevolence. A person must first care for others, have affection and love, even pity regarding the human soul before it is possible to command power and the understanding of when to kill. Mencius and Confucius agreed that a rule of men is "Benevolence."

4. Politeness is the epitome of Japanese culture, even today, which astounds many foreigners who have become lax in their proper decorum. Rooted in benevolence is courtesy of all and therefore, being polite is acceptable of a true man. True politeness is not a worry of fear of offending others, but having feelings for others—caring about them, even if they are

strangers. Politeness's highest form is love, according to early writers of the Samurai code.

5. Sincerity and honesty, also known as Makoto, says if a warrior thinks they will act then it will be completed. There is nothing that would stop a Samurai from completing a mission or action. It was known that a Samurai would not have to give their word or make a promise and that all they needed to do was an act. It was known that a warrior would always carry out a task and never lie because a true warrior does not fear the truth, but embraces it.

6. Honor is combined with worth and dignity both as a profession and in personal situations. A sense of honor comes from being born to value the duties and privileges offered in one's job. For the Samurai disgrace was a constant fear. A true Samurai would show patience for the most unbearable acts.

7. Loyalty is the seventh virtue a Samurai needs to have. Yes, it loyalty for those they were indebted to, but also to the code of honor. A gang of thieves would still be allegiant to their leader—if they had loyalty. It was a matter of personal fidelity within their circles.

8. The last and perhaps the most essential virtue of a good Samurai was self-control. Controlling one's impulses is imperative to keeping one's morality in check. To be able to adhere to the other seven attributes, you need to be able to control your actions, when and how you act, as well as what is right or wrong. The Samurai believed in knowing what was right, such as when to kill because of being offended and when to let a person go because of benevolence.

Chapter 4:
What Makes a Good Samurai

The eight virtues of the Samurai should tell you most of the answers to "what makes a good Samurai?" However, there are still some things that need to be explored to help you understand why they are revered today, as much as in the past.

Samurai rose out of necessity. Japan needed warriors that could fight battles, stave off invasions, and protect the "main" culture of Japan. Of course, we can always look at what this means—one race thinks they are superior to another. Someone else wants to lead versus the person who is currently in charge. Does this make the motions of one better than the other?

It is an existential question that may never have an answer. If we consider that at first one in four men were drafted into the military, then we know the laws of the Samurai had yet to start. But, in seeking a better reputation, it was necessary for the warrior to come up to a code that could raise their status above others and make them more than road robbers given government backing.

Again, through necessity, the warriors needed to change, if for nothing but a new image. This gave rise to the people we revere as the noblest warriors, at least when discussing Japan.

If we also consider that during this same time, Western countries had knights with their code of ethics, then it appears the human race as a collective felt it necessary to uphold certain beliefs with regards to the men who fight.

Even today, we can look at the soldiers who sign up to protect countries and discover that many of them have a particular moral compass that says killing is okay, but under the right circumstances, with the proper ethics being met.

Soldiers wish to protect their homeland, not necessarily a person, but a group of people. Samurai needed to fight on behalf of their masters, go when they were told and to fight when they were told. Today, soldiers go where they are told, but may not have full faith in the "master" they serve, rather a thought of justice. The concept of freedom has taken over as the masterful reason to fight versus a single person or ruler.

But, enough digression. The point is not about today versus then, but what makes a warrior capable of following on an "enlightened" path that promotes justice.

You will agree that certain things are morally acceptable. If a group of people is raising an army to take your land, you have the right to defend it. If someone is working to overthrow the government you have because it is corrupt and hurting the majority of people in your country, then fighting for a better government is correct. These are the points the Samurai had to weigh, in addition to doing as their master commanded.

Without thinking about whether any one person or group of people can truly decide what is best for everyone, it is possible to assess the eight virtues of the Bushido code and determine that they are the best descriptions of a good person, as well as Samurai.

Consider a working situation. If you work for a company and your employer shows you loyalty, by giving you pay rises, increasing your duties, and depending on you, are you going to stab them in the back? No, the just person is going to help this person and continue working for them—show them the same loyalty.

If a person is not catching on to something at work, will you show them kindness and benevolence, or will you dismiss them? A good Samurai will know there are limitations for certain people, but those people still deserve compassion. Benevolence is working with them, seeing where their potential lies and creating a way for them to be effective.

There are literally hundreds of examples that can be provided when discussing the eight virtues, rather than going through all of them—know that a good Samurai is one that does not falter.

Self-control in all aspects is the only way for a person to be a good Samurai. If you have a belief system and code, you cannot waiver or change your mind to fit any situation. For example, a good Samurai is going to swear loyalty to his master, and not question their requests, unless it goes against the moral code. If someone is asked to murder, without reason, without justification a good Samurai had to weigh the reasons and follow through or terminate the employment.

This concept goes back to the saying our moms and dads had for us as kids, "If someone jumps off a bridge, would you follow?" It is meant to be an ethical question. Yes, you might feel loyalty for that person, but if you know it is inherently wrong, then you must step back and not follow. The Bushido code offers the same directive.

Through Zen Buddhism and Confucian teachings, the Samurai was supposed to be better at making the proper decision regarding right and wrong. It gave rise to Ronin, like the story of the 47. They had a master who died, due to offending another. The offense was something they did not see as just, so they obtained justice. But, in the end, they had to follow through with their code and join their master using seppuku.

Now, we can all argue the code of following the master as being wrong. Having 46 or 47 skilled warriors kill themselves, took a great many men away from the army, but as was their code of honor, they made a promise and kept to it.

So, what makes a good Samurai is:

1. Following the eight virtues.

2. Being a learned person capable of making choices that are morally correct.

3. Having the courage to stand up to immoral acts.

4. Keeping your self-control in all situations so that you can follow the other seven virtues.

5. Never wavering in your belief in the code.

The fighting warriors known as the Samurai may be gone, unneeded in the way they performed in the earlier centuries, but their lessons about behavior and being above reproach still apply.

Chapter 5:
How Can You Learn from the Samurai Philosophy

Good news—you are already learning from the Samurai philosophy. You are researching the Bushido code, getting explanations for how it started and how the Samurai followed their beliefs. The next thing is to weigh situations and see how the Samurai philosophy would apply.

Self-control is the hardest aspect of the Samurai code and one that most people have trouble adhering to. Restraint is about creating moral conduct that will go above logic. Samurai were men of action, so it was the Samurai's job to teach character, such as prudence, language, and intelligence, but above all be a person of action. A Samurai could choose compassion over confrontation, benevolence instead of violence, but always act when necessary. What is right is always going to be right and what is wrong will always be wrong. The Samurai who has the self-control to avoid doing what is wrong and still follow the righteous path has plenty to teach us.

For example, what would you do if you were twenty feet from the next crosswalk and you wanted to go to a shop on the other side of the street? You see no cars are coming, would you cross, knowing it was jaywalking? The person with the Samurai's heart, would go to the crosswalk and wait for their opportunity. The person who has no self-control will cross. This second person thinks it is okay because they are not hindering traffic, but rules are rules. Of course, you could argue that the rule of jaywalking is not ethical in the first place or a "moral" rule you need to follow, but that is not the point. If you accept the laws of the country you live in, then you cannot pick and choose the rules you want to follow.

Let's take a harder question. If someone drops a hundred-dollar bill on the floor and you know who it was, do you rush after them to return it or keep it? The moral person and the Samurai would return it. The person who doesn't have a moral compass would keep it.

What about foreclosure? Would you rob a bank to save your home from entering foreclosure? Most people would not. They would either work out a solution or file for bankruptcy losing the house, but they would not go as far as robbing a bank.

To learn from the Samurai code, you have to establish that there are legal rules based on moral and ethical principles that should never be broken. Even if you are born into those rules, without the control of setting them, they are still something you must follow.

So, in one respect, your self-control to maintain the rules of the world you live in is paramount to learning what it was to be a Samurai. The next is about following other teachings that support the Samurai teachings.

Zen Buddhism

Buddhism is often thought of as a religion, and perhaps under the strictest definition, it can be. However, if you read through the principles of Buddhism, it is more of a way of life. There is not a celestial being that you praise or pray to, but rather an enlightenment you attempt to reach as a way of becoming better and helping others be a more significant person.

Zen Buddhism is the Japanese version of the Asian religion. It has a few changes that make it slightly different, but helpful when considering the moral and ethical compass one should have.

Buddhism is part of the virtues of the Samurai. In fact, some of the principles from Buddhism are applied directly to the type of person you should be if you are going to be a warrior. There is one difference between the practice of Zen Buddhism and being a Samurai.

Buddhists inherently believe you should not harm others. Killing even the smallest insect is against their moral beliefs. The Samurai was trained to defend and kill for the greater good of their people, to raise an army against another who would attack, even if they did not attack first.

So, with one slightly "large" issue, many of the other qualities of a Buddha have been kept. Buddhism teaches a person to reflect on their actions and thoughts, to meditate and let come what is "known" versus what we believe or can see.

Within the confines of Buddhism, which are not many, people are asked to meditate, to let their thoughts go, and maintain peace. It is to use intellect versus belligerence, fear, and killing to attain peace.

Buddhism also believes that one should rely on oneself and reflect on the more significant questions about why someone could have so much and suffer, while another has little and is happy. The original

Buddhist gave up his kingdom to travel the areas around him to find the answer. What he offered in the teachings is for people to give up material things, to be kind, generous, benevolent, courageous and self-disciplined. As you can see, there are correlations between the eight virtues and Buddhism.

To become a Samurai or even to learn from the Samurai's philosophy, you must also embrace Buddhism. Try to do no harm, act kindly towards others, and forget about the material belongings of the world.

Confucius

Confucius provides the world with Confucianism, a religion practiced first by China, then by Korea and Japan. It began in the 6th century BC and provided analects texts that are filled with rituals and traditions. Some see Confucianism as a philosophy versus religion, and again it would come down to the definition of religion. Most religions have a god or several deities that are prayed to and depended on.

Being a good Samurai meant following Confucianism principles like benevolence, loyalty, reciprocity, filial piety and ritual norms. According to Confucius, these laws provide De or virtue. As a belief system, Confucius believed there was a heaven or T'ien, which was a positive and personal force within the universe. He was also very optimistic about human nature and their potential.

Confucianism is about following ethical principles versus rituals and practices like other religions, which is another reason that many consider him a philosopher versus a religious leader.

For the teachings of the Samurai, you would need to understand the full texts of Confucius, follow his ethical boundaries, and believe that there is a state of being that raises you above others, so your soul can be free from the earth and live in a state of nirvana.

If you can learn the principles of Confucianism, Buddhism, and follow the virtues of the Samurai, then you have learned all you can from their time of life and would mainly be a Samurai without the need to fight.

Chapter 6:
How Can We Apply Bushido to
Modern Life

Despite being an advanced culture, with technologies Samurai could never dream of, their principles can be applied to modern life in various ways. Already some examples of how to use the Bushido code to modern life have been given. But, let's look at all aspects of life.

Personal Application

Buddhism tells us to give up material things and to do no harm to others. Think about some recent incidents in your life. Were there times when you were not as lovely as you could have been? Were there things that you could have helped with, but you did not?

For example, at Christmas, did you donate clothing, food, money, or time to helping others? If so, did you do it because you felt obligated or because another person needed help? You see, we like to think we are being selfless, without the need for kudos coming our way, but are we?

Many of us feel obligated to do something nice. If someone buys us a Chai latte because they want to, we then feel the obligation to purchase next time. When someone asks for help with a charity event we often do it because there is a benefit in it for us, such as getting free food after the dinner is over.

The right self-less person, who follows Confucianism, Buddhism, and the Bushido code does not look for satisfaction in the things they do. Yes, it may be there, but the ultimate goal is not to feel obliged or wish for the "thanks" to be given.

By working on your selflessness, you can achieve a more uncomplicated life, where you are loyal and benevolent, without the need to be thanked anytime you do a good deed.

There are also steps you can follow to live a more disciplined, selfless existence with a little material hold on the life you lead. The essential lesson is to embrace what is around you, the lessons that the Bushido are providing you with these words, and apply it. When you get to *how to live a better life*, you are going to see some of the steps we are talking about.

Professional Application

Like in your personal life, you can apply the eight virtues to your career. Imagine working for a place, where there are two owners. The first owner is the one on record, and the second knows he will receive the business as an inheritance and he holds a position as the second in command. What would you do if you had the brother of the owner tell you to call him the next time the cops or FBI come looking for him? Could you morally feel like it is a company you could work in or would you know that it is against your nature—your very virtues to continue working for a criminal?

For the Samurai, they were taught to be loyal to their masters. But, they were also shown the code for knowing what is right is right and what is wrong is wrong. Ethically, calling up someone who is wanted by the cops or FBI and tipping him off, would be against the rules of man. One could argue it would be loyal to do as the employer asks, but again, if you have to sacrifice your ethics and what is correct, then there is no choice. You would not agree to do such a thing, nor would you call this person when the cops arrive. Instead, you would tell the police that the person in question is not at the place of work and if it is the truth—you do not know where the person is. If asked to call the person by the police, would you do it?

Here is the next dilemma. The Police are asking for your assistance to call the person and see if you can get his location, but is this your job or should they be the ones to go to his home and other known hangouts? The answer is—the police should do their work and allow you to do yours. You are under no obligation to make a phone call and try to gain the person's whereabouts, nor should you give that person a heads up that cops are looking for him. You have done what you can to maintain your own Bushido code.

Of course, most of us are not faced with such a drastic situation. But, there are others that are regularly shown in movies. What about the accountant working for a company who finds an error. The accountant first reports it to the owner, thinking the person needs to know, and it is also a moral obligation to report such findings to the police. However, do you report it, or do you let the owner know? Loyalty says you let the owner know there is an issue. In the movies, it is often the owner skimming from his accounts, and thus one is lead on a thrilling ride. So, as a fiction question, you would then have to turn the owner in to the police and save your life? In the real world, you would want to follow up and make sure a report is made, but you also have to be one hundred percent certain that it is not compromising the loyalty you have for the company. There are ways to check this, such as seeing if a report is filed, and keeping up with the owner as to the solution. Whenever there is a question of right and wrong, you go with your Samurai teachings and know in your heart that what is right is the moral challenge to turn over all evidence of misconduct to the proper authorities, as the owner should wish to do.

Even the smallest thing can be done in your professional life to apply the Samurai code. A customer comes in and does not have enough money to buy something, you discount the item, and the person can leave. It is morally correct to do this. You are helping someone who is down on their luck. You are also supporting the business reputation. You can even decide to repay the till with the money or seek your employer's opinion if you did the exact thing they would have done in that situation.

As with the application of Bushido in your personal life, numerous examples can be given. These are just a couple of things for you to consider and work towards. You are also going to see some steps that will help you in your professional life to adhere to the Samurai way of thinking.

Chapter 7:
How to Live a Better Life

Living a better life, overall, requires a balance between work and personal life. It is also about changing your perspective. If you have a cynical view that is rooted in materialistic things, it is going to be more difficult for you to live a better life.

The first step is achieved given that you are looking for a way to follow the Bushido code and live a better life.

Now let's see what else you can do to gain what you want to attain. Desire is often considered an unethical emotion and one that you should not have. But, even the Samurai desired to follow a more righteous path, to be necessary and offer skills that helped their masters. In life, we are unable to live without "wants." Even the need to live a better life using the Samurai code is as much a necessity as it is a desire to achieve this goal.

Self-Discipline

Your way to a better life starts with self-discipline. Of course, it should since this is the very virtue that ties all eight together and makes the Samurai. Self-discipline is necessary for your personal life as it is in your professional one. To make a good impression we often show that we are intuitive to the needs of our employers. We jump on tasks that need to be done and show that we do not need direction in most instances.

However, when we get home and see the tasks before us, we tend to let them fall by the wayside. We also get complacent in the workplace doing the minimum without putting in the extra effort.

To live a Samurai existence, one has to embrace self-discipline in everything. Begin by setting yourself tasks and completing those goals. At first, you can go about an easy option, such as cleaning when you get home from work instead of letting the dishes or dirt pile up for another day. As you gain more discipline to accomplish tasks, make them more prominent goals.

Get into a routine that keeps you on track as much with goals as with the virtues you wish to uphold. The control to avoid your impulses assures that you will fulfill the essential duties first. The Samurai can have self-control automatically.

For example, if you know you watch too much TV, instead of doing other tasks, then you must push yourself until you are completing all goals first before rewarding yourself. Your soul requires this consistency. There is a line you do not want to cross in allowing your inner self to rule for only your gain.

Minimalizing Life

The next step in your path to living a better life is the realization that material things are unnecessary for your happiness. This is a Buddhist teaching as much as it is a part of the Samurai lifestyle. You should not dwell on money or things you want from stores. Instead, you should accept what you have and enjoy the people around you. Living a simple life with payment being food was what the Samurai did. They did not become wealthy for their gain. Instead, they fought, protected, and followed virtues to ensure a comfortable existence. Being paid in rice helped their families live and the warriors to survive as they moved from place to place keeping the peace.

When you accept that you can be happier without the things you have around you or money to buy what you so desire, then you can focus on family, friends, and the simple life. You can stop wanting a new book, journal, movie, couch, TV, or other material things. It also allows you to enter a place in your mind where you can get rid of the items you do not need. If you have ten pairs of the same pants or shoes, a TV in every room of your home, or a thousand books when you have only read 100 of them, you know there are things you can eliminate to declutter your life and be happier.

Never Lie

Lying has become acceptable. It may be the white lie that is amenable, but it should not be. The Samurai taught us that lying is not good. One needs honesty in life, where you make a promise and keep it never stepping out of your honorable line.

A white lie can hurt someone. Omission is an area that you need to understand. If you omit something, it does not mean the other person will not feel you were not lying. The one thing you need to do to be a Samurai is, to tell the truth, no matter how painful it is for you. It takes courage, to tell the truth, to uphold a promise, and to only agree to the things you know you can.

If you think about lying, then check yourself. If you know you are not going to call a friend later, then do not say you will. If there is a chance that you will not be able to call this person, do not promise to do so. Even this situation can be a lie. Lying is part of the Buddhist approach that lent to the Bushido code. Buddhists tell the truth despite how hard it can sometimes be.

The key to leading a better life overall is your happiness and understanding what it hinges on. It can be different things to different people. For example, one person can be happy being near family, helping out when needed, and staying at home with minimal contact with the outside world. For another, happiness is having children, a family, and making sure they are supported.

As long as you dwell on the negative life is going to be difficult. You have to want to live in a positive world, where the things you have are enough. When you can attain this, you will live more like a Samurai, who is noble and just. You will show future generations that you can be honest, courageous, honorable, and maintain self-control.

Can you help me?

If you enjoyed this book, then we really appreciate it if you would post a short review on Amazon. We read all the reviews and your feedbacks will help us improve our future books.

If you want to leave a private feedback, please email your feedback to: feedback@dingopublishing.com

Thanks for your support!

Now, let's continue on next page

Conclusion

The Samurai were not myths. They were not legends to be found only in movies. They were men who started with regular beginnings and rose to fame. Some were peasants; others were sons of earlier warriors. But, what has caught our attention is the code they lived by.

It was quickly established that to become honorable and rise above the typical belief regarding men of war that the Samurai warriors needed to live by specific rules. These virtues included courage, honesty, loyalty, self-control and four other traits that many did not possess.

The belief system rose on the backbone of Buddhism and Confucianism, showing that men of war could be intelligent as well as strong enough to defeat their enemies. What made the Samurai mythically was their ability to die an honorable death, without holding a grudge. Oda Nobunaga took his life rather than face a dishonorable death at the hands of his enemies. It was revered for a man to gut open his abdomen and die. It was even acceptable for the head to be cut off and then to receive an honorable burial.

Today, the world is lacking a great deal of what the Samurai held deal. Honesty is seen not as a virtue, but something that can keep one back. Courage is only for those who fight in the war and not for the regular person. Self-control is being replaced by the attitude of "I want it now, and thus I will take it."

Learning about the Samurai is a perfect way for you and anyone else to go back to the roots of chivalry and learn why it was important. Hopefully, you have gained knowledge for why chivalry is not a myth and why it needs to be employed more now than ever. It is not about holding the door for women or treating them with kindness. No, chivalry is about having honor, loyalty, honesty, courage, self-control, and knowing what is right is right. It is about looking at the black and white, not the gray that we believe exists.

The last lesson of the Samurai is to employ the virtues in your life to live a better life not for yourself, but for the future generations. When we are in an era that is all about "me" it is time to show that there is more outside of one's self.

Before you go

We have a surprise for you!

As a way of saying thanks for your purchase, I'm offering a special gift that's exclusive to my readers.

http://bit.ly/VBonus1

Another surprise! There are free sample chapters of our **best-selling** books at the end.

1. **Life in Japan** by James Walker (Page 58)

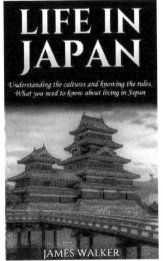

2. Australia: History of Australia by James Walker (Page 107)

More books from us

Ramen Noodles Cookbook by Linda Nguyen

Pho Cookbook by Linda Nguyen

Kale Cookbook
by Olivia Green

Chia Seeds Cookbook
by Olivia Green

Anti-inflammatory Diet For Beginners
by Jonathan Smith

Intermittent Fasting
by Jonathan Smith

HIIT – High Intensity Interval training
by Joshua King

Anti-cancer diet
by Olivia Green

Bonus #1

Sample chapters of Life in Japan by James Walker

Introduction

Japan may be one of the smaller countries, set on an island, but it has a diverse culture, a dominant financial center, and long, varied history. Japan is 145,932 square miles in size. As globalization grows, more people become fascinated with life in Japan, its past, and the pop culture. Manga, Anime, Sony PlayStation, and so much more has become highly desirable by people around the world. It is little wonder that a book about the history, culture, lifestyle, and living in Japan is necessary to explore all that such a tiny country offers.

From a time of some of the most significant warriors ever known to the tumultuous period during the World Wars to now, Japan has shown the world that it is possible to be small and succeed.

Whether you are interested in the culture of Japan, the rules and language or more of the way of life one can enjoy on the island; it will all be available.

In the end, you are going to understand the best and worst of Japanese living, as well as if you can afford to move there and enjoy the history, diverse landscape, and people of the island.

You are going to fall in love with Japan, perhaps hate it a little sometimes. You will be able to enjoy a vacation or live there, confidently knowing you have explored all you can in written form before arriving.

Chapter 1:
History of Japan

The history of Japan would take a book itself; however, it is possible to give a short introduction to the periods in history. These eras are listed:

1. Early Japan

2. Nara and Heian

3. Kamakura

4. Muromachi

5. Azuchi-Momoyama

6. Edo

7. Meiji

8. Taisho and Early Showa

9. Postwar

Early Japan is up until 710 AD. The second period ends in 1192, with the Kamakura period ending in 1333. The Muromachi era lasted until 1573, with the Azuchi-Momoyama a short thirty-year affair. Edo is perhaps the most well known as it is often depicted in shows and movies (1603 to 1868). The Meiji ended in 1912 when the Taisho and Early Showa took over between 1912 and 1945. Today, Japan is said to be in Postwar.

Some of the critical elements of Japan are the Jomon, who is the first Japanese to live from 300 BC on, becoming the Yamato, Ainu, and Ryukyuan. Rice was introduced in 300 to 250 BC as an essential staple.

Tombs were first erected from 250 BC to 538 AD, during a time known as Kofun.

In early Japan, during the Asuka timeframe, Buddhism was introduced from China, and the seventeen articles of the Shotoku Constitution were designed.

Nara was the first Capital of Japan, which was established in 710, but only 74 years later, the capital was relocated to Nagaoka. During the Nara and Heian period, the capital moved again to what is now Kyoto. Power changes also occurred where the Taira Kiyomori clan took over political decisions. It was also a time when the Jodo Sect of Buddhism was formed, and the Minamoto clan ended the Taira leadership.

Zen Buddhism began in 1191, and the government would change a few more times, giving rise to the legal code called Joei Shikimoku. Mongols also tried to invade Japan in between 1274 and 1281.

For a small period during the Muromachi period, there were southern and northern leaders, due to a fight in which the emperor fled to Yoshino in southern Japan. However, before the 1300s was over the two courts were unified again. The Portuguese sailed to Japan in the 1500s, introducing Christianity and firearms. It is also the century when Nobunaga rose to power as one of the most revered Samurai.

Japan tried to invade Korea during 1592 to 1598 but was unsuccessful. There were also plenty of warring states in Japan, with the fall of Hojo and Tokugawa defeating rivals at Sekigahara.

During the Edo period, the Tokugawa government was in power in the new capital of Edo, or what is now Tokyo. Christianity was persecuted, and one shogunate clan was wiped out when Osaka Castle was seized.

Japan was extremely isolated during this time, eliminating a lot of trade with Korea and China. They also closed their borders to Western travelers. Many Koreans became enslaved if they tried to enter Japan without the proper documentation. Towards the late 1700s, Russia started negotiating trade and finally, Commodore Matthew Perry forced Japan to open ports for trade.

The Meiji Era was a time of great feats and war. In 1872, the first railway built, running between Tokyo and Yokohama. The Sino-Japanese and Russo-Japanese wars occurred, and there was the annexation of Korea in 1910.

Japan became part of the allied forces in 1910 during World War I. After the war, Tokyo and Yokohama had to recover from the Great Kanto Earthquake.

During the Showa period, the Manchurian incident occurs, with the second Sino-Japanese war starting six years later. The Second World War began, with Japan on the opposite side, instead of backing their moves to destroy the US, with Pearl Harbor's destruction. It was a period when hate was definitely abundant, with Japan trying to win, killing thousands, and winding up surrendering after two atomic bombs destroyed Nagasaki and Hiroshima. Until 1952, there was an allied occupation of Japan, and four years later the country joined the UN. Relations with China become normalized in 1972, and a year then there was an oil crisis.

However, during the later 1900s, Japan started producing many electronics, cars, and other items desired by Western countries. It helped Japan rise as a financial power, being listed in the top five countries.

Throughout their history have been earthquakes, Tsunamis, and devastating choices in wars. But, Japan is continuing their financial domination exporting more than they import, keeping the budget on the positive side instead of a deficit. Their trade relations are also better for oil needs.

This is not to say that Japan has not suffered some financial setbacks, but they do continue to show intelligence in how they regulate the foreign currency market and banking system.

The US continues to keep military relations with Japan, although, there are some negative thoughts about keeping a US base on Okinawa. Talk in the most recent century was asking for the US to leave or at least dwindle their numbers, but a resurgent problem with North Korea and its nuclear weapon program has again changed these talks.

Japan and South Korea continue to run war simulations together to show their power as a means of controlling actions by North Korea.

Major Economics

Japan is the third largest auto industry and holds a high ranking for innovative global patent filings. In 2015, Japan held an estimated $13.5 trillion in financial assets and 54 of the Fortune Global 500 companies. Japan keeps much of their financial assets in the private sector, which also affects the countries wealth and caste system. Regarding the GDP, Japan has the highest ranking of public debt, with the national debt predominately in the private sector.

Japan has gone nuclear-free, regarding power plants, switching to natural gas. The country also depends mostly on rail transport. About 84% of Japan's energy is imported from other countries, but they are looking towards hydroelectricity for renewable energy and lowering their dependency on other countries.

For industries, manufacturing, real estate, and wholesale/retail trade are the highest percentages providing the GDP numbers. Other services and activities, such as agriculture and tourism, are the top category.

Fitness and Work

Japan has worked to increase the health of their people by offering better working environments, despite the long hours. Many industries in Tokyo, require workers to remain on the clock for twelve hours, with the first 20 to 40 hours of overtime going unpaid. The work culture has usually been for long hours, but many are beginning to fight this when their contract states eight hour days. Japanese people grow up with the thought that they will have 100 hour work weeks, but in saying this, there are compromises with longer holiday allowances.

Companies are also adding in ways to help their office employees remain physically active, such as the treadmill desks and providing rooftop gardens. These are not always provided, but they are becoming more normal.

The correlation between work hours and pay is sometimes skewed. For example, a pilot can earn

$143,000 or 17,121,000 yen. They usually work 138 hours in a month. A medical doctor working 174 hours earns closer to 11,540,000 yen, so less than a pilot. Jobs such as crane workers, nurses, and factory workers work anywhere from 170 to 200 hours for as little as 4,000,000 yen or $35,680.

So, the history of overworking employees, from the earliest of times until now, is that many are working long hours, but their culture does not complain. They know what they are accepting when they take an offer, and it is imperative for them to choose a job they will love or have temporarily.

Chapter 2:
Culture of Japan

Japanese culture is varied from what many Western countries understand. A great deal of what we think we know comes from pop culture, and to a degree, it is accurately depicted. However, once you visit Japan and live among the people there, you will see the diversity and the belief that life can be enjoyable, as well as filled with challenging work.

Not everything in Japan is perfect of course, but there are certainly lessons that can be gained from the current culture.

Starting with pop culture, some people walk around with their hair painted assorted colors, such as blue or red to pay homage to their favorite anime or manga. But, everyday life is generally filled with long work hours and an eye towards fitness.

To understand the culture of Japan, it is better to look at the past and work our way to the modern aspects you will see on a visit to the country.

Three Japanese Culture

Japanese culture includes Samurai, Geisha, Japanese gardens, tea ceremonies, and kimonos. The culture has roots in Chinese culture, but historically, there have always been differences between the two due to the land mass separation. Japan also enjoyed extended periods of isolation prior to their enforced segregation later. Certain aspects of China were imported, overwhelming the Japanese with Chinese culture, but it did not take long for a distinctly Japanese style to arrive, which is often seen the gardens and temples.

It is imperative you understand that there are three distinct cultures in Japan and it is offensive to lump everyone into "Japanese." Like "Westerners" have diversity, Japan has primarily three cultural groups: Ainu, Ryukyuan, and Yamato.

The Ainu, pronounced Aynu, are indigenous to Northern Honshu, Hokkaido, and a few islands north of Hokkaido. There are genetic differences between Ainu, Ryukyuan, and Yamato.

When it comes to religion, the Ainu follow distinctly different concepts than Buddhism and Shinto. They still worship gods, as if they are elements of nature. The Ainu also have animal and plant gods.

In the 1700s, when the cultures of Japan started mixing, it was clear to see differences in the clothing worn by the Ainu versus Yamato and Ryukyuan. The housing choices also differed, with bark, grasses, and bamboo used to construct their homes. Houses were seven by five meters, which is approximately 23 by 16 feet.

The Ainu are primarily isolated today, preferring to keep to themselves much as they did in the past. A CNN travel piece says some guides work at a museum, but they are wary of tourists and typically quiet sharing only a little about their heritage. Some Ainu live on Sakhalin, near the east coast of Russia and in Honshu, which is Japan's largest island.

Estimates put about 24,000 Ainu people living in the world today. Their language is a mixture of native and Japanese, with only about ten people still speaking fluent native Ainu language.

The Ainu are known for their brutal hunting methods of animals. They still revere bears and wolves, but hunting is normal. Deer are also a significant source of meat for them. The fact is— Ainu use techniques from their past to hunt, which can be against most of the worlds animal rights.

This area of Japan was harsh for a living, and it still is. The Japanese government did not recognize the Ainu as indigenous to Japan until this century. The ten-year anniversary of recognition is in 2018.

Still, between 1868 and 1912, there was a movement of a more global Japan. This period is referred to as the Meiji Era when mainstream Japanese heritage was more integrated with the distinct cultures like the Ainu.

Education is critical to raising awareness of the Ainu, and it is said that the Ainu cultural center in Tokyo will be ready for the 2020 Olympic Games. Inside the new facility, people will be able to learn about the traditional dress of the Ainu people, their hunting methods, and struggles to live in a modern world. It is not to say that there are no current buildings in Northern Japan; however, there are still traditions followed that come together to create an exciting landscape.

Ryukyuan

The Ryukyuan live mostly on the islands of Okinawa and the Ryukyu islands. There are also some northern islands they inhabit. There are numerous sub-groups of Ryukyuan's including Okinawans, Amamians, Yonagunians, Yaeyamans, and Miyakoans. Each of these groups has specific dialects. Like the Ainu, Ryukyuan people have distinct religious beliefs, architecture, and clothing. Their clothing is not as different from mainstream Japanese as the Ainu.

There was the Ryukyuan Kingdom that was taken by Satsuma in the 17th century. The Ryukyuan culture spread throughout more of Japan due to the overthrowing of the kingdom, but lately, genetic studies place Ryukyuan and Ainu as more genetically linked than the Yamato. The Ainu are stocky, fairer, and have Caucasian elements.

It is also known that the Ryukyuan had ties with China before the Japanese colonization of the Meiji Period.

With regards to religion, the Ryukyuan follow traditions and legends that relate to ancestor worship, meaning they respect the living, dead, gods, and spirits, with a little worship of animals. There is influence from Chinese religions, including Taoism, Buddhism, and Confucianism. Ryukyuan has in some instances adopted the mainstream Shinto religion. One of the ancient aspects of the Ryukyuan religion is their onarigami belief, which is the spiritual superiority of females. They believed in priestesses or the Noro system. It is a system derived from the Amamikyu. Many of the shamans and mediums were female.

The most dominant culture of Japan is the Yamato people. About 98% of the population is genetically linked to the Yamato. It was not until the 1800s that the term Yamato Japanese was used to show the distinctions between the three-distinct people of Japan. It was related to the incorporation of the Empire of Japan, with the Yamato Dynasty running the Imperial house from 660 BC. The Yamato people have ruled in each of the significant dynasties, periods, and kingdoms of Japan.

As the world continues to find the primary origin of "humans," archeologist do believe Japanese people were on the island before the formulation of Chinese and Korean cultures. However, it is not a concrete theory. There are definite differences between Japan, China, and Korea, but also enough to show that hunter-gatherers migrated to the island from northern and southern Asian locations.

For the Yamato, Buddhism was the primary religion, and it continues to be the same today. They are also responsible for building the tomb culture for the aristocracy during the early Kofun cultural period.

It is the Yamato who adapted to the changes in the world, starting with hunting, gathering, and fishing, they also adopted technologies from other parts of the world through trade to encourage innovations.

Examining the Samurai

Part of the history and culture of Japan are the Samurai. The term was first applied to written works in the 900s; however, it is known that warriors existed prior to this time. The Asuka and Nara periods, which coincide with Tang China and Silla in the 660s, are when Japan required military reform. The Taiho Code of 702 AD was formed as part of the restructuring of the military to create a military that would be able to fight. Emperor Monmu also established a law during these periods that 1 in 3 to 4 males would be drafted into the military. They would need to bring their weapons but would be exempt from taxes and duties.

The rise of the Samurai is marked by the late Heian period, around 1160 AD. Samurai fought in a naval battle showing their prowess. But, it was Emperor Kanmu who established the title of Shogun in the 8th century or the early Heian Period.

Geisha

While talking of groups of people, the Geisha is also a necessary discussion on the culture of Japan.

Many myths are surrounding the concept of Geisha, perpetuated by pop culture such as the movie *Memoirs of a Geisha*. The Geisha is a woman, who follow a distinct line of discipline, beauty, and grace. The word "geisha" translates as an artisan or performing artist, but it is meant to indicate a high-class professional, trained in traditional entertainment. Geisha attend to guests at banquets, parties, and meals often demonstrating their skills with the shamisen. They are meant to initiate games, conversation, and more. Usually, they serve in tea houses, ryotei (traditional restaurants), and are paid a fee.

It may surprise you to learn—the first geisha were men. They started working in the 18th century, and it was not until later than females began occupying the position of geisha. In the 18th century some geisha did start offering sex as part of the entertainment; however, the oiran geisha became less popular and Japanese men began asking for a high-class companion there to act as hostess instead of a more intimate friend.

So, if someone says geisha are prostitutes it is more accurate to say they are oiran and geishas are highly-skilled entertainers who go through a great deal of training. Geisha did have personal relationships with patrons, but today the tradition is to be separate from their danna regarding a more intimate relationship. They are there for financial reasons to be hostesses. In the past, it is possible young girls were sold to geisha houses (okiya) for reasons of poverty; however, today all geisha make it a career choice.

Geisha do primarily make their money by being hostesses for men or mostly male-dominated parties; however, working in restaurants, they also provide care for women. It should also be understood that the mizuage is a ceremony that was performed by courtesans and prostitutes in the past, but it did not involve the maiko, which is apprentice geishas. Maiko is young, starting training at 15, 16, or 18 depending on where a person lives.

Geisha do have specific hairstyles, ornaments, makeup, and dress that they follow. The traditional clothing is the kimono. The makeup is a full white face for maiko only. Geisha only wear makeup in an exceptional performance. The hair ornaments are meant to be decorative, with simple combs or kanzashi ornaments. The hair is highly skilled, using wigs to provide the elegant styles. However, many geishas are turning to natural hairstyles like the maiko trainees due to hair loss. The last part of the costumes is the footwear, which is usually high wooden sandals for maiko and shorter wooden sandals or geta for the geishas.

While the tradition was once prevalent, many of the geisha work and live in Kyoto, but it is harder to find people in Tokyo performing in this position. About 1,000 to 2,000 women are currently working as geisha throughout Japan. The exact number is difficult to pin down due to a lack of study in the small cities. Kyoto shows an employment of possibly 300. It is also hard to pin down the number since some are a maiko, studying to work as artisans, but may not follow through with the same high-class artistry as the "geisha." Training has opened for non-Japanese who wish to learn the discipline and principles of the geisha. Maiko can also be taken into work as a helper, doing errands, but unless they make a formal public debut, they will not be "official."

Kimonos

It should not surprise you that what we take for granted as traditional Japanese clothing, to epitomize the culture of Japan, was just the word for "clothing." The style of Kimono that we recognize as the conventional geisha dress was the way they made clothing in the late 700s AD. As clothing making became more developed the style of apparel increased. At first, separate upper and lower garments were constructed, as were one-piece outfits to ensure a person was thoroughly covered and warm.

Adding layers to clothing started in the 12th century, where bright colors were added to represent different classes. Now what we know as the kimono is worn for special occasions like funerals, weddings, tea ceremonies, as a matter of employment in entertainment fields.

Japanese Gardens

Japanese Gardens are part of Japanese art, and they have taken on a life of their own around the world. Numerous cities across the globe and the USA, in particular, are creating Japanese Gardens to bring the culture, heritage, and relaxation of these landscapes to the people. Many cities hire renowned Japanese artists to provide all the elements a garden should have.

Historic Japanese gardens are spread throughout Kyoto and Tokyo. The difference is that many of the gardens in Kyoto will also have shrines and historic temples. They even change with the seasons, with colorful foliage in the fall and beautiful Sakura blossoms in spring.

Two things go into these heritage sites: time and nature. It takes time for the gardens to grow naturally, with little help from the caretakers. Japanese gardens usually symbolize gravel or sand to show rivers, while other rocks are meant to depict mountains.

Japanese merchants during the Asuka period (538 to 710) would visit China, bringing back Chinese arts, including gardens. Buddhist monks continued with this tradition, as did diplomats, scholars, translator, and students. The gardens first appeared in the 7th century.

The oldest style is called Paradise, and it was created during the Heian period. The Sakuteiki is a book written on the tradition about the Japanese technique and still revered today.

With the flourishing Zen Buddhism belief during 1185 to 1573, the concept of the Zen garden was produced. Zen Buddhist temples incorporate this style. There are specific elements that make it a Japanese garden of any persuasion, including Zen.

- Water

- Gravel

- Sand

- Stone

- Island

- Rock

- Hills

- Teahouse

- Stream

- Fish

- Bridge

- Strolling paths

- Stone lanterns

- Bamboo pipes

- Flowers

- Moss

- Ponds

- Trees

- Gates

- Statues

- Garden architecture

- Garden Fences

- Water basin

As long as some of these elements or all of them are found in a garden, it is considered a Japanese Garden.

Like the cultural differences between races, there are also three main types of Japanese gardens: Karensansui (Zen), Tsukiyama and Chaniwa.

The Zen Garden is a spiritual location, with sand or gravel representing the sea or river, rocks to show mountains and islands, and few small trees. It is a place for yoga, meditation, or just observing the patterns made in the gravel.

The Tsukiyama is a hill and pond garden, filled with the lush mossy landscape, complete with water, bridges, fish, trees, stones, hills, flowers, and small plants.

The Chaniwa is the tea garden often accompanied by a tea ceremony house. There is an inner and outer garden, with a covered gate, lantern style figures, and water basin or tsukubai for washing your hands. There are also stepping stones in the tea garden.

There are other non-traditional gardens, like the newer courtyard garden. These gardens allow current people of Japan to have a little place to relax and enjoy nature, with their favorite elements.

Japanese Tea Ceremonies

The Japanese Tea Ceremony is an essential element of traditional culture. It can be called Chanoyu, Ocha, or Sado. It is a ritual ceremony preparing and serving Matcha, and traditional Japanese sweets. Preparing the tea has predefined movements throughout, including how to pour the tea in front of someone. It is not about drinking the tea, so much as it is about the aesthetics, preparation, and the feelings of one's heart. The host has to consider the guest with each movement and gesture. The tea utensils are placed at specific angles for the guest's viewpoint.

Tea was first brought into Japan during the 600s AD. However, it was in the eighth century that a formal ceremony was created. Japan was somewhat forced into the building and cultivating their traditions around tea because of its rare and valuable connotations. Tea was challenging to get at first, with China holding on to their seeds and the nobility preventing lower class people from gaining it as a regular beverage.

The ceremony adapted overtime, with a Zen Buddhist erecting a temple and serving tea as part of the religious purposes of the location. He also suggested that the leaves be ground before adding the water. Later Hui Tsung, a Sung emperor, mentioned the addition of a bamboo whisk to stir the leaves. Grinding the leaves and using a whisk are two necessary elements to the ceremony you will see in tea houses throughout the world, and particularly in Japan.

The qualities of a proper server are those who have faith in the performance of the tea, who act with decorum befitting a master, and those who have practical, excellent skills.

Japanese Language and Dialect

Japanese has dialects, which helps others pinpoint the region a person may be from, as it does in any country. The origins of the language are unknown but thought to be rooted in the Altaic language family, like Turkish, Mongolian and other Asian systems. There are also some similarities in Austronesian languages, notably, Polynesian.

Writing Japanese varies by the character sets. There are three: Kanji, Hiragana, and Katakana. When writing Japanese, one can write in horizontal rows from the top to the bottom of the page or in traditional style creating vertical columns, going right to left on the page.

Grammar for Japanese is simple, without too many gender articles or plural/singular concepts. However, there are some conjugation rules for verbs and adjectives.

Pronunciation is how the language makes its mark. Japan has few sounds, which makes it easier to learn. There are also fewer homonyms, in which words are pronounced in the same way, but have different meanings. In Chinese, you would find one word can mean more than two things.

The important aspect about Japanese is the level of speech you use. It is necessary to use honorific language or Keigo when you are in formal situations. As a Westerner, you would be expected to use formal language and rules versus talking like a friend or you would to a child.

Chapter 3:
Lifestyle

In Japanese history overview, it was clear to see that employment is a significant factor in the Japanese lifestyle. According to some news reports, people sleep perhaps 35 hours a week and work around 100 hours. It makes it difficult to understand how such a culture, who seems to live only for work, can have a lifestyle.

It is precisely the work ethic that demands a view of a lifestyle that completely separates the Japanese and many Asian cultures from Western countries. Yes, work takes up most of the time, but there are other benefits, such as company meals, fitness during working hours, and fun.

Are there some downsides—yes—rumors and studies show issues with mental distress. But, then again, one has to consider if all the facts are supplied. The cultures of Japan view depression and other mental health issues with different stereotypes than Western cultures, even to how they see suicide. Thankfully, recent studies are showing that mental health needs to be more mainstream regarding correcting it, and the country is slowly moving out of the dark ages. Unfortunately, there is still a stigma about mental illness, even depression that prevents people from seeking help. For suicide, on a global scale, Japan has one of the worst problems.

Perhaps, it can be argued that if you work long hours, despite some of the nicest working conditions and amenities, you still feel the weight of the world on your shoulders.

For tourists, it may be easier to look at what Japan can teach us about living longer, healthier lives, as studies show many Asian cultures do in comparison to Western countries. For people who want to live and work in Japan—you will need to change your viewpoint on what it means to work.

The Diet

Japan is heavily invested in seafood diets. The National Marine Fisheries Service shows 55.7 kilograms per capita of seafood was consumed in 2016. In comparison, the US ate 24.2 kilograms. People who eat a lot of fish tend to live healthier lifestyles because there are different cholesterol levels in fish versus meat. In fact, there is a 35 percent lower risk of heart disease in people who eat fish as a primary protein. Omega 3 fatty acids are linked to several types of cancers, which shows that fish can help prevent these issues, as well as inflammation. Some studies prove eating fish can enhance the mood due to obtaining Omega-3 fatty acids.

Another aspect of the Japanese diet that helps with a healthier lifestyle is seaweed. The UN numbers show 100,000 tons of seaweed is eaten each year by Japanese people, with 20 different species used in their cuisine. Seaweed can offer 2 to 9 grams of protein per cup. Seaweed is also known to regulate estrogen and estradiol levels, helping to reduce breast cancer in woman.

Japanese cuisine is centered on seafood, raw and cooked, okonomiyaki, noodle dishes, and chicken. Japan is also reputed to have better beef, Kobe.

Fermentation, of food, is another favorite part of the Japanese diet. Several of the side dishes offered on menus are pickled. Soy sauce, miso, and natto are also helpful in keeping one health since it helps with one's digestion. Adding miso paste to your cooking can help break down food before it reaches your lips, thus giving rise to a better immune system.

Entertainment

Japan is big on entertainment. Karaoke is one of the top pastimes for Japanese. There are at least 229 locations for Karaoke in Japan for just one chain, Big Echo. Around 20,000 men sing and go drinking with friends after work, and they show an improvement in cardiovascular health versus those who do not go out singing.

Overall, entertainment is a big industry in Japan. There are various bars, with and without karaoke, and company meals are part of the package. Social support is tremendous for most people working and living in Japan, not only as a way to build better teams in a working environment but also to keep healthier.

Whether, you enjoy manga, anime, or games, studies are also showing that letting your inner "fun" person out is going to do you good. Japan takes this as serious as they do their long work hours by offering clubs, for gaming and dressing up as characters.

Another aspect of the Japanese lifestyle is laughing and being silly. A lot of the shows, including drama and reality television productions, are incredibly, over-the-top silly. They also offer commercials, Westerners find silly, but the studies come back with laughter being a good dose of medicine. Laughter is known to release endorphins that reduce pain, alleviate depression, and increase one's immune system. If you live in Japan, be prepared to see silly things you might consider "stupid," and yet find you cannot help but watch. You cannot be serious all the time; especially, working 80 plus hour weeks.

Exercise

Keeping fit is an essential part of the lifestyle. Not only are fitness options provided at work, but there are places for yoga, meditation, and relaxation too, which keeps people energized.

Japan provided a 16th national holiday called Mountain Day. It celebrates mountain climbing and helps bring the concept of forest therapy alive. Forest therapy is exactly what it sounds like—going out in the green forests around the cities and enjoying nature, recuperating and exercising. Being outdoors, helps people gain vitamin D, which is necessary for energy. Not getting enough vitamin D is known to lead to autoimmune disorders, cancers, and arthritis. By spending time outdoors in quiet forests, researchers show a 20 to 50 percent improvement in cognitive function.

It is not a bad way to look at the Japanese lifestyle and know you want to take part in it. Being healthier, simply by living more like the people of Japan is a possibility.

Bathing

Japan is also reputed to have some of the best baths in the world. A part of the lifestyle is the public baths and hot springs. About 85 percent of Japanese people spend their end of the day in a bath. During the 17th century, numerous written texts expounded on the reasons for a hot soak to stop illness. There is something to this line of thinking, since baths, particularly in hot springs, are full of minerals that help with skin disorders, rheumatism, and neuralgia. Those who meditate during baths also see a drop in blood pressure.

Tea as a Staple

Japanese citizens also make tea a part of their lifestyle. No, you do not have to have a tea ceremony every day, but just make tea. Drinking five cups of green tea per day can lower mortality by 26 percent, according to one study. There are also correlations with improved cognitive function and reduced heart disease risk.

********End of sample chapters********

Life in Japan by James Walker

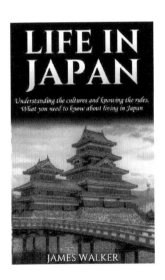

Bonus #2

Sample chapters of Australia – History of Australia book.

Introduction

For generations in schools, both in Australia and in many other parts of the western world, students were taught that the first settlers in Australia were the British. This has been shown to be incorrect. One reason is that on the coast of Western Australia DNA testing has proved that there is European ancestry in some of the Aboriginal tribes in both the northern and southern areas.

In fact, there are a number of aboriginal people living in these isolated areas who have blue eyes, some with blond hair and some even have very fair skin coloring. These people can trace their parentage back to times before the first know landing of Europeans in Australia, so the question is, how did they manage to have European ancestry. Nobody knows, although there is a lot of speculation it may have been early sea travelers like the Vikings 700 years before Captain Cook sailed into Botany Bay in 1770.

Chapter One:
A Brief History of Australia

The first humans to discover Australia travelled there by sea around 60,000 years ago. Being mainly nomadic and living from hunting as well as gathering their food they were able to easily adapt to living in almost all parts of Australia.

Early in the fifteenth century, many European countries were exploring the world looking for new lands and riches such as gold and other precious metals.

The Dutch were one of the most adventurous and aggressive of the early explorers; they believed there were many areas in the southern hemisphere where gold could easily be found.

The first of the Dutch sailors in these southern waters, William Jansz in 1606 discovered Cape York in what is now known as Queensland Australia. When they landed, they thought the place was very inhospitable with its snakes, large crocodiles, sharks and stinging jellyfish. The natives they encountered were also not very friendly, so he did not stay long.

Around the same time other Dutch ships were sailing the Australian waters, they reported that most of the west and northern areas were barren and lacked water making them of little economic value to the Dutch. They named the country New Holland and "Terra Australis Incognita" which translates to Unknown Southern Land.

Willem Janszoon was the first (Dutch) European to document his meetings with the local Aboriginal People as he sailed and charted the east coast in his ship "The Dyfken".

It has been estimated that there were at least 54 European ships from a number of different countries visiting Australia between 1606 and 1770. One of these ships was captained by Able Tasman, a ship like many of the ships sailing the southern hemisphere that time, owned by the Dutch East Indies Company.

Able Tasman charted much of the coastline of Australian and later, had several areas named after him including the Tasman Sea and Tasmania

The famous English man, Captain James Cook in his sailing ship "Endeavor" mapped the east coast of Australia and then on the 22 of August 1770 he claimed the east coast of Australia for the English King, George III and named it New South Wales

Captain Cook then sailed southeast and discovered New Zealand and many of the islands of the South Pacific.

Other explorers such as the English mariners Bass and Flinders made detailed maps of the Australian coast with the help of the French mariner Baudinmd. They discovered that Tasmania was a separate island.

There were a multitude of explorers all around Australia at that time and many areas have been named after them. Some well-known examples of this are; Arnhem Land, Torres Strait, Tasmania, Dampier Sound, the Furneaux Islands, La Perouse and Cape Frecinyet.

Chapter Two:
The First Fleet and the Start of a
New British Colony

When the first British immigrants arrived in Australia they were not properly prepared or equipped for living in Australia, they expected conditions to be similar to the areas they had left in England. They came in 11 ships commanded by Captain Arthur Phillip that held a total of 13500 people including the crew and passengers.

They landed at Botany Bay between the 18th and 20th of January 1788 and found the area was not suitable for building their settlement. The seeds and plants they had brought with them did not suit the climate and so they relocated to Camp Cove Port Jackson on 26th Jan 1788

Captain Arthur Phillip was made Governor and had instructions to build the first British Colony in New South Wales. He found that they were totally unprepared and had neither the equipment or food supplies needed. They made friends with the local Aboriginal people, started trading with them for basic food and with them, developed farms in the Parramatta region about 25 kilometers inland on more suitable land.

When the second fleet arrived with badly needed new supplies and equipment in 1790 it made things much easier for the struggling first colony.

This second fleet was supposed to bring new settlers and convict labor for the colony, but it was known as the "Death Fleet" because the living conditions during the trip were so bad that 278 of the crew and convicts died on the voyage.

The colony had a difficult time because of the climatic conditions they encountered, lack of provisions and basic food stocks. There were also social problems because at that time in the colonies there were four times as many men as women.

Contact and Colonization

The area of Albany was claimed in 1791 by George Vancouver creating a new British colony in Western Australia for King George 111.

Generally, when the first European explorers arrived in Australia and met with the native or Aboriginal people they found them to be friendly and easy to get on with.

Once they managed to communicate and started trading they found the Aboriginals were very interested in some western items like axes, knives and shiny trinkets. The aboriginal people also liked blankets, but were not very interested in clothes, as they did not wear them.

Governor Phillip was very active in gaining the help of the Aboriginal people for farming, hunting, fishing and trading. They at first were very cooperative, but then when they discovered the settlers were taking their land and excluding them, they became understandably hostile.

There were many confrontations when the aboriginals were either just killed or driven away from the areas being farmed and settled by the colonists. In the Sydney area the "Eora" clan and their leader Pemulwuy of the Bidjigal planned and undertook a series of attacks designed to frighten off the settlers between 1790 and 1810.

The Governor responded by placing a bounty on any aboriginal found in the areas where the colonies were located, dead or alive. The government also gave out licenses to shoot Aboriginals on sight, which caused any remaining Aboriginals to flee the area. The last of these licenses was revoked in 1957.

Chapter Three:
New South Wales, The Law and Land

New South Wales started as a penal colony in 1788 and remained that way until 1823. Its population was made up of a small number of free settlers that came on the early ships, but mainly convicts, their guards and marines as well as some of their wives. A few lucky convicts became guards because of their good behavior, this was unpaid, but they had their sentences reduced. Once the convicts had served their prison time they were released and allowed to settle where they chose.

118

The British government established in 1823 the first New South Wales Parliament, first they set up a Legislative Council and then the Supreme Court. Under an act of The English Parliament in London; it was known as the 1823 New South Wales Act (UK). This was the very first step to creating a new Government in Australia. It gave the free people and the convicts both criminal and civil courts to air their grievances.

The indigenous land owners were not recognized by the government until the 1830s when there were two land treaties signed between John Batman and the Kulin people for 600,000 acres of land between Melbourne and the Bellarine Peninsula.

This, for the first time, acknowledged that the Aboriginal people owned the land and had the right to sell it. Sir Richard Bourke, the NSW Governor was not happy about this arrangement as it would set a precedent that others would follow. He issued a proclamation that stated that all the land of Australia belonged to no one before the British crown had taken possession of it. It further stated that all land now belonged to the British Crown.

The British Colonial Office agreed with Governor Bourke and issued another Proclamation that stated that "Any person found in possession of any land they did not have the express permission of the government to occupy would be treated as trespassers."

They also stated that the crown owned all the land claimed by Captain Cook on 22 August 1770, under instructions from King George III of England. Before this claim, the land was owner-less, even though the "House of Commons" had recognized in 1873 that Aboriginal occupants had the legal rights to their land.

The law stated that in order for anyone to claim a title to any land they first had to purchase it from the government whether they were Aboriginal or from another country.

This ruling from 1830 was used in the Australian courts until 1992 when the High Court recognized the traditional land ownership and rights of the Australian Aboriginal in the "Mabo" Lands Rights Case in 1992.

In 1861 The Crown Land Act permitted any person, regardless of their country of origin to select and get a title to a section of Crown land of up to 320 acres of to settle on.

The conditions were that a suitable deposit had to be paid and they had to occupy (live on) the land for at least three years.

This Crown Land Act had the effect of limiting the Aboriginal people's right of access to these newly formed pastoral and farm lands. Up until this time much of this land was the traditional home and hunting lands of the Aboriginals who lived in those areas.

This opening up of the land to new settlers resulted in many conflicts between the various groups who were competing for the land. This included the new landowners, the Aboriginals who were living there, various squatters and the government agents who were charged with selecting who could claim the land titles.

Huge areas of what was vacant land was now being claimed, this caused many disputes and resulted in a relatively large number of people becoming fugitives from the law. Some, because they missed out on getting a property, turned to a life of crime, such as the famous bushranger and highwayman "Ned Kelly".

Other people tried to use elaborate schemes to swindle others from their legally obtained property, they were known as bushwhackers.

Despite all the problems people faced, the former penal colony of New South Wales grew and prospered. The area where the first British Colony started, The Port Jackson Settlement is now Sydney, which has become Australia's largest city.

Chapter Four:
Other British Colonies in Australia

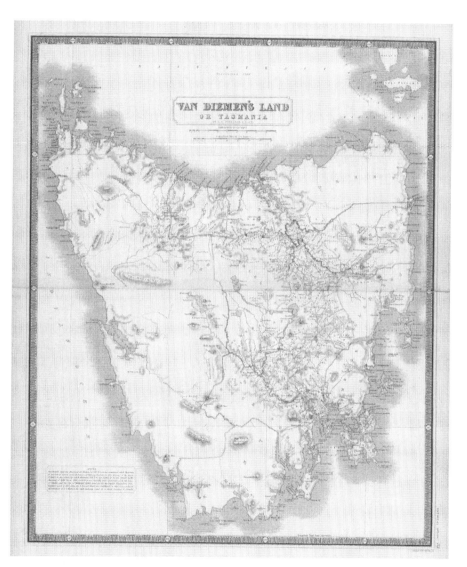

Van Diemen's Land

Tasmania was originally known as Van Diemen's Land. At Risdon, Lieutenant John Bowen landed a small group to establish the first British settlement on the island in 1803. The group was made up of former sailors, settlers, convicts and soldiers, but this site was soon abandoned in favor of a new site. Lieutenant David Collins established a new settlement at Hobart called the colony of Van Diemen's Land in 1825. The Government officially changed the island's name to Tasmania in 1856 after the explorer Able Tasman.

Western Australia

The first British settlement was built at King George's Sound (Albany) Western Australia in 1827 by Major Edmund Lockyer. Two years later the Swan River Colony had its first Governor, Captain James Stirling. In 1849 it became a British penal settlement with the first group of convicts arriving there in 1850.

South Australia

The British province of South Australia was first established in 1836 and became a crown colony in 1842. Although there are a large number of ex-convicts settled in South Australia it was never used as a convict colony. By 1850 there were over 38,000 immigrants and ex-convicts living there.

Victoria

Lieutenant David Collins made the first attempt at settling Victoria in 1803, but because of the extremely harsh conditions they encountered there, the settlers were forced to settle in Hobart Tasmania in about 1804 instead.

The Henty brothers landed in 1834 at Portland Bay to start a settlement that was eventually to become the City of Melbourne. When John Batman settled there the Port Phillip District became officially sanctioned. Port Phillip's first immigrant ships arrived in 1839.

Victoria and the Port Phillip District officially separated from New South Wales in 1851.

Queensland

The Moreton Bay Settlement penal colony at Redcliffe was established in 1824 by Lieutenant John Oxley. It then moved to an area that is now known as Brisbane with about 2,280 convicts sent there between 1824 and 1839. In 1838 the first of the free European settlers moved to the district, soon to be followed by many others. Once the city of Brisbane was established it split away from New South Wales to separate into individual state called Queensland.

Northern Territory

The Northern Territory was originally like most of Australia, part of the New South Wales penal colony. The first European settlers that went there established themselves at Fort Dundas, Port Essington in about 1824.

South Australia took control of the area in 1863 and in 1869 Palmerston Town which was later known as Darwin was established as its capital city.

The Northern Territory became a part of the Commonwealth of Australia on 1st January 1911 when it separated from South Australia.

****End of sample chapters****

Australia: History of Australia by James Walker

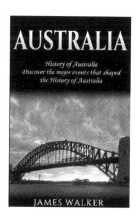

Thanks again for purchasing this book.

We hope you enjoy it

Don't forget to claim your gift!

http://bit.ly/VBonus1